The Great Accelerator
Paul Virilio

Translated by Julie Rose

polity

First published in French as *Le Grand Accélérateur* © Éditions Galilée, 2010

This English edition © Polity Press, 2012

Polity Press
65 Bridge Street
Cambridge CB2 1UR, UK

Polity Press
350 Main Street
Malden, MA 02148, USA

ISBN-13: 978-0-7456-5388-4
ISBN-13: 978-0-7456-5389-1 (pb)

A catalogue record for this book is available from the British Library.

Typeset in 12.5 on 15 pt Adobe Garamond
by Servis Filmsetting Ltd, Stockport, Cheshire
Printed and bound in Great Britain by MPG Books Group Limited, Bodmin, Cornwall

The publisher has used its best endeavours to ensure that the URLs for external websites referred to in this book are correct and active at the time of going to press. However, the publisher has no responsibility for the websites and can make no guarantee that a site will remain live or that the content is or will remain appropriate.

Every effort has been made to trace all copyright holders, but if any have been inadvertently overlooked the publisher will be pleased to include any necessary credits in any subsequent reprint or edition.

For further information on Polity, visit our website: www.politybooks.com

Contents

To the illuminists of light-speed
at CERN, Geneva,
and
to the Wall Street traders who crashed into
that other wall, the time barrier.

The Insecurity of History

To live every instant as though it were the last —
that is the paradox of futurism, of a futurism of
the instant that has no future. We might note
that it also spells the decline in the propaganda
of an endless Progress that, only yesterday, still
fuelled the history of past centuries. That history
is now so wired, so hysterical, that it even claims
to foresee actions, the reality of events that have
not yet occurred. You'd think that, tomorrow,
we'll be able to construct an actual 'History of the
Future' – thanks to long-term forecasting. Such
micro-narratives would impose themselves on the
historicity of the avowed facts, as if the perspective of the real time of instantaneity suddenly
annulled all durability. For, thanks to certain

software programs and the modelling they allow, the mythology of futurism is even gearing up to renew the myths of our origins and of Antiquity.

A recent anecdote might serve to illustrate this 'phase transition' in History: at the beginning of the Year 2010, Bernard Accoyer, then president of France's *Assemblée Nationale*, protested against the excessive use, by the French government, of a speeded-up process that limits both parliamentary chambers' examination of proposed new laws to a single reading.

'We can't go on working this way – not if we want decent laws and decent democratic debate', Accoyer declared, adding that he would not hesitate, if the need arose, to resort to the possibility of opposing the emergency process in question by siding with his opposite number in the Senate, Gérard Larcher. 'A good law', Accoyer concluded, 'requires an incompressible period of time for reflection.'[1]

The current legislative frenzy actually introduces the inertia of real time, a paradoxical inertia that results from the sudden acceleration of common reality.

1 *Le Monde*, 11 February 2010.

In these very early years of the third millennium, the polar inertia produced by the instantaneity of interactive CONNECTIONS (*LIENS*) is actually poised to supplant the fixed-property inertia of PLACES (*LIEUX*) – including the most representative places of legislation and the law. The whole of historicity will then find itself shattered by this 'distortion of competition' between the past and the future that is so detrimental to the present, with the NANOTECHNOLOGIES of the infinitely short term already taking the place of the traditional chronologies of the medium and long term of past days, years and centuries.

All of this undermines the sovereignty of History – and the sovereignty of all anteriority, with it. So, following the age of territorial insecurity,[1] comes the age of the insecurity of History and its tripartite division, PAST – PRESENT – FUTURE.

This reversal of values, we might note, has already affected space. At the close of the last century, geopolitical strategists were, in fact, turning reality inside out like a glove and asserting that, forever after, the *exterior* was to prevail over the

1 Paul Virilio, *L'Insécurité du territoire*. Paris: Galilée, 1993.

interior. Today, it is in the order of *time* that this turnaround is being accomplished, as posterity is primed to dominate all anteriority. Hence the sudden insecurity of History that now complements and completes the insecurity of a territorial sovereignty now threatened on all sides – from above, by its expansion, and from below, by its regional fragmentation. Hence the 'repeat delocalization' we are currently witnessing under the pretext of globalization, along with the impact of a process of externalization – outsourcing – that is increasingly untethered to any practical reality.

In any case, the current debates between historians over MEMORIAL LAWS, codified bills dedicated to the memory of specific victims of historic crimes, clearly point to the damage done by 'progress' regarding the notion of historical anteriority and its great narratives, which are in the process of disappearing. What is rising to the fore in their stead is what certain people are already calling the 'great national novel'.

So, what we are now seeing, after the topographic and geometric effraction of distances, is the anachronistic effraction of the time intervals required for effective knowledge as well as for memory of the facts. FRACTALIZATION of physical expanse is coupled with fractalization of durations relative to the CONTINUUM of a general History that's in the process of being instantaneously obliterated.

Let's hear what Winston Churchill had to say on the subject, when he addressed the House of Commons on 13 May 1940. If a battle between past and present is allowed to break out, Churchill said, there will be 'no survival for the urge and impulse of the ages, that mankind will move forward towards its goal'.[1] In other words, we'll lose the future.

We know what came next: Great Britain as a space did not suffer the insult of occupation, but only because the British leaders avoided a chronopolitical battle over the TEMPO of the Battle of Britain.

That was an odd lesson in history; but it was also a lesson in geopolitics, in which the perspective of the CHRONIC temporality of events was undefeated by the prospect of the panicky instantaneity behind a 'futurism' whose fascist origins were all too obvious, starting with Marinetti's

1 Winston Churchill, *Address to the House of Commons*, 13 May 1940.

tracts celebrating the Great War as 'the world's hygiene'. The cult of the acceleration of history ended appropriately enough for the futurists in the Blitz, that lightning war of the failed invasion of the sky as well as of the British Isles.

As for us, if in the near future we let some Museum of the History of France settle permanently, whether in Paris or somewhere else, we will very swiftly find ourselves occupied – and extremely preoccupied . . . Maybe we are already.

Everyone knows that time is revealed and then revolves, is gone. The REVOLUTIONARY of bygone days is now about to be eliminated by the revelationary forecaster, the REVEALER of postmodern times.

Apropos the 'systemic crisis' in the TEMPO of the stock market and in the future of an illusion, that of getting the world economy back off the ground, some people are already flagging the alarming development of *distortion of competition* for single-market turbocapitalism. And it's happening right where the dromologist would insist on the term ANAMORPHOSIS for the temporality of the instant, as most clearly describing this financial façade that can no longer be seen except by watching images on STOCK EXCHANGE screens, and, then, only from a particular angle: that of the curved distorting mirror of the roundness of the terrestrial globe – in other words, the continuum of an accelerating 'globalization of affects' by traders operating in a market that's now, once and for all, interconnected through PROGRAM TRADING, through the synchronization of an interactivity that makes a whole new kind of insider trading possible.

Let's be clear about this eccentric angle on the world economy. In the last quarter of last century, the City of London launched market interconnection, the BIG BANG of program trading, so aptly named. That was to lead, as early as 1987, to an inaugural crash implicating the real-time computerization of trading. Twenty years later, with the bursting of the subprime real-estate bubble in the United States in 2007, it is the flash trading involved in high-frequency exchanges that has been stigmatized by the Securities and Exchange Commission (SEC), the Wall Street watchdog, considering the accruing risks of a new kind of insider trading. For, distortion of competition now resides in the instantaneity of milliseconds in a stock market NANOCHRONOLOGY that escapes market control – this, smack bang in the middle of the credit crunch and massive loss of investor confidence.

BIG BANG, BIG CRUNCH. In the absence of any true political economy of speed, one dealing with the wealth of the developed nations, these events lead to a relativist felony, an extremely serious distortion of competition in a market that is no longer single in the real time of stock market exchanges, even if it remains single in the real space of the globalization of profits. The capacity of a few big banks to engage in flash orders, using computing power analogous to the power of nuclear deterrence in the hands of the top brass of the military, calls into question the very basis of free competition in a turbocapitalism clearly nearing its end.

This, I think, explains the importance of the term ANAMORPHOSIS in relation to temporality and to the sudden temporal compression of financial data before the curvature, the distorting mirror, of the continuum of an economic history that resides today in the astronomical TEMPO of an instantaneity and an interactivity that once and for all spurn the old laws of a competitive market where the felony of insider trading, perpetrated by cheats, was still committed within the common historical TEMPO of the chronology of days, hours and seconds – not within the NANOCHRONOLOGY of nanoseconds, picoseconds or femtoseconds of an 'information bomb' that is currently in the process of exploding before our very eyes.

Here, the anamorphosis of free trade is produced by the anachronism of this sudden futurism of a real instant that exploits the criminal operation of digital systems and their deviant 'mathematical modelling', willy nilly. And does so at the risk, this time, of exhausting confidence, the speculative faith of shrewd investors and shareholders, along with credit, in a BIG CREDIT CRUNCH (fixed property-based or other), since, as we all know, confidence can't be instantaneous or automatic.

Hence the major risk of a *choc de la confiance*, a 'crash of confidence', as devastating as the *choc des civilisations*, the clash of civilizations, with the ATHEISM of the free thinker suddenly turning into an atheism of free trade, in the age of banks that are too big to fail, but, especially, too swift to be honest!

Ultimately, this disastrous situation ought to

cause us to wonder about the nature of a new inertia: the inertia of Time, of the real instant and of the interactivity involved in the transactions that take place within the Single Market, fostering the growing risk of a monopoly that would be damaging for all kinds of exchanges. This would be a MONOPOLY OF DISBELIEF and of an 'atheism' in which the loss of speculative faith would most likely end in a sort of MONO-ATHEISM of the Single Market that would be analogous in its evocative power to the MONOTHEISM of religions, of the single God of justice and truth.

So, that would be it, the 'systemic' risk, the integral accident in high-frequency speculation, where the inertia of real time would take over from the real-space inertia of settlement according to the nations' *emploi du temps*, their scheduling of time – *timetables* – in the several-thousand-year-old era of the sedentary homebody.

Let me just summarize: if the *emploi du temps*, the timetable, behind historical chronologies, the tripartite division past–present–future, were to completely disappear, overtaken by the accident of an overwhelmingly anachronistic instant, then the NANOTECHNOLOGIES of futurist instantaneity would soon lead to loss of memory and abandonment of History's credibility to the detriment of all confidence in the future. The contemporary world of the globalized Single Market would then end in a POLAR INERTIA of unequalled atemporary passivity, an inertia of the real instant. And that inertia would, this time, totally shatter the notion of the duration and sedentary stability of planetary settlement, since the inertia of the interactive instant would soon completely outdo the fixed-property inertia of activity in the real space of humanity's routine daily life.

As for the geographic and, so, 'spatial' aspect of this development, seen through the anamorphosis In competition mentioned above, it would be flagged by loss of confidence in the notion of Progress and by the overwhelming prevalence of delocalization of production – but also of research and development. For, URBAN EXODUS, in the twenty-first century, will one day reproduce the agony of RURAL EXODUS, in the age of the industrial revolution in transport and lead to the headlong rush – only, *in closed circuit* – of a general exodus of humanity.

Last century, French Air Force general, Lionel Max Chassin, declared: 'The fact that the Earth is round has not yet been taken into account by the military.' It seems that today's economists and financiers of the Single Market still refuse seriously to entertain that fact, certain of them even asserting that progress in communications has made the world perfectly flat,[1] like some multimodal logistical platform! Hoodwinked by the reality effect of accelerating profits, the speculators of the moment are so mesmerized by STOCK EXCHANGE screens, they apparently don't notice the deformation of values caused by the curved mirror of stock trades in the age of globalization and, so, the 'astronomical' nature of this sudden time compression that, of course, allows them to make highly impressive profits. But only at the cost of more and more fragile 'bubbles' that will soon produce the SYSTEMIC CRASH of turbocapitalism and, more than anything else, the SECURALISM of speculators who will no longer be able to have confidence in the future of the illusion

1 Thomas Friedman, *The World is Flat.* Harmondsworth: Penguin Books, 2005.

of progress or to expect the latest software to
deliver the miracles promised by the mathematical modelling used by a market subject to the
excessive speeds of hyperactive flash trading.
The relativist felonies committed by the insider
traders involved in high-frequency electronic
exchanges will suddenly put the brakes on the
hyperliberalism of the Great Casino, quite as if
the speeding-train effect of high finance escaped
traders and, especially, the Nobel Prize winners
in economics – apparently unlike the planners
who laid out the railways – as though the insecurity of History wasn't bound, some day, to
fatally meet head on the insecurity of the ter-
ritories involved in the nations' *emploi du temps*
– our timetables!

Actually, the virtual Great Casino of the third
millennium looks a lot like those geostationary
satellites in orbit above some locality or other and
whose fixed-property inertia is said to be geosyn-
chronous in terms of the verticality of a given
PLACE, whereas the polar inertia of the financial casino is CHRONOSYNCHRONOUS
with every place on the globe thanks to its
instantaneous interactive connections.

So, though it may be single in the real space

of geography, the globalized market is no longer single in the real time of trades involved in the flash trading perpetrated by the insiders of the 'Big Night' of the Stock Exchange. The above-mentioned distortion of competition created by hypervelocity will suddenly trigger the trans-mutation of capitalism, or, more precisely, the phase transition of the turbocapitalism of an overwhelmingly critical instant. For, traders who are fans of flash orders will, this time, trigger the accident to end all accidents of a stock market tempo that is now AUTOMATIC. The loss of awareness of all true duration will trigger the loss of confidence, the credit crunch of the latest investors, speculative faith having once and for all evaporated.

Surely we can't fail to notice that this is hap-pening! The very notion of a kind of capitalism fuelled by capital from somewhere else, out of sight of any true production and based on weight-less speculation, is nothing more than a market lure, an economic aberration that leads straight to the dreaded systemic crisis – like those hedge funds whose accounts departments are exiled these days in offshore havens, fiscal paradises, where they are managed by what often comes down to some minuscule team that can work in an apartment, the speculative fund having no real legal status.

Insecurity of territory, with the importance of islands, of offshore venues and the evidently waning importance of, say, Switzerland, along with banking secrecy . . . Insecurity of History, whereby the accounting standard of the market is on the point of replacing the historical standard of the listing of stocks on the Stock Exchange . . . These are all so many clinical symptoms of the 'futurism of the instant' and of its impact on economic intelligence in the age of an ecological disaster whose scope never stops spreading in broad daylight.

In a recent interview published in the *Sunday Times*, the chairman and CEO of Goldman Sachs, Lloyd Blankfein, declared: 'I'm just a banker doing God's work.' Clearly, this particular God is no longer hoping for much from his faithful profit-worshippers, the investors to whom the Messiah of finance could still say, on account of the abundance of their speculative faith: 'Go, your faith has saved you!'

Actually, the credit crunch, the crisis of

confidence, that has hit the stock exchanges of the Single Market, is just an early-warning sign of a true ACCIDENT IN KNOWLEDGE that is about to strike an 'exact' science which has recently turned into a technoscience of instrumental efficiency that bears no relationship to the knowledge we've acquired over the course of the ages. That technoscience's sophisticated mathematical models and software don't dissimulate all that well the systemic catastrophe of a science that has no conscience, a science that no longer even sees the warning symptoms of its own decline and especially not the limits it has now reached in its discoveries – at once atomic, informatic and genetic. More than anything else, the 'digital civilization' so often trumpeted marks a return to numerological paganism and its cults of yore.

Actually, the world of the pharaohs of finance is not flat as they claim. It is miniscule, infinitesimal – just like the degree zero of a technical Progress that would no longer fool anyone, without its propaganda. So, with the breaking and entering into the instant, the fractalization of historical TEMPO, the NANOTECHNOLOGIES behind the reality effect open up the unheard of possibility of trumping the economic with the astronomic. When that happens, the science of the ecological *habitat* will really shake up the *habitus* of societies once settled in sedentary fashion, with the routine nature of our daily timetables, our *emploi du temps*, being totally abolished. The ACCELERATION of flows of all kinds will then supplant – this time for good – the historical ACCUMULATION of stocks of wealth, of goods once housed in that reservoir, the city of men.

If this were effectively to happen, the current delocalization of production would in no way lead to some future relocalization of activity, industrial or otherwise. It would lead to a definitive EXTERNALIZATION – OUTSOURCING – of the urban race, right here on this tiny telluric planet – until salvation came in the form of some other 'promised land', this one EXOPLANETARY, the single-file exodus of the biblical epic yielding to the looped exodus of a circus prophesied, in a way, by the circular accelerator in Geneva!

The virtual *otherworld* of cybernetics is, in fact, nothing more than the anachronism of an *othertime*, in which the critical space of Mandelbrot's 'fractals'[1] merges with the critical instant of a fundamentally uninhabitable continuum. That continuum is just the anamorphosis of the practical reality of a forgotten topography, since the repetition of all our movements, as well as of a nation's actions (their political liturgy), registers a lot more forcibly in the domiciliary fixity of 'sedentary man' than in the headlong rush, the forced exile, of unbridled 'nomadism'. Hence the urgency of a question that is now central or, more precisely, terminal: the question of the nature of INERTIA, in the age of the revolution in information and the apparently unremarked transference of the FIXED-PROPERTY inertia associated with the real estate of PLACES – *LIEUX* – to the POLAR inertia of CONNECTIONS – *LIENS*. For, twenty-first-century interactivity now dominates the standardization of behaviours and activities that characterized both the nineteenth and twentieth centuries. And that domination entails an increased ECOSYSTEMIC risk of paralysis or, rather, the sudden tetraplegia of a societal body whose perpetual motion is

1 Paul Virilio, *L'Espace critique*. Paris: Christian Bourgois, 1984.

frozen in each of its limbs and whose structural unemployment is now a self-fulfilling prophecy.

This mass unemployment is forced on us partly by the automation of postindustrial production and partly by the automation of reflex actions in our now outrageously speeded-up *emploi du temps*, our agenda. That is the impetus behind the much-touted threat of relaunching the world economy – except that, this time, such a relaunch would be without any *emploi du temps* whatsoever and would occur within the cybernetic space defined by the inertia of the propitious instant – the right moment – for supernumerary man, a man decidedly without qualities . . .

In the United States, for instance, the drop in the wage bill in the last quarter of 2009, coupled with an unchanged level of activity, does indeed signify that American firms are improving productivity – but only to the detriment of employment. That fact clearly points to a future deindustrialization of nations, as a prelude to which the current delocalization of firms in favour of low-cost employees is nothing more than an early-warning sign of the spread of automation. Tomorrow, the robotics of artificial intelligence and its 'enhanced reality' will take on the bulk of productivity in a resolutely post-modern world.

In the face of this assessment of affairs and for want of a political economy of speed and not just of the wealth of nations, the 'speed box' (gearbox) of technical progress will go into automatic mode and the stock market crash brought on by speculation will end, sooner or later, in the crash of all job production. The futurism of the instant requires it and will force it tomorrow on the generations to come.

HERE is no more. Everything is NOW, and the *HIC ET NUNC* of days gone by is about to disappear completely from the horizon of history. In his recent *vade-mecum*, French public intellectual, economist, banker and top-tier consultant, Jacques Attali recommends 'living every moment to the hilt as though it was the last'. Attali even goes as far as declaring that, 'Since time is the only really rare commodity, it is now the only one worth being saved.' That is why, he reckons, it is urgent 'to focus on every instant'.[1]

---

1 Jacques Attali, *Survivre aux crises*. Paris: Fayard, 2009.

A symbol of a fatal inertia, this verbatim account illustrates perfectly the inexorable nature of this delirious futurism that deconstructs all chronology and, with it, the melody line of history as well as the great narrative of our common memory. This is what really lies behind France's recent spate of memorial laws and the growing threat to territorial identity of a nationality that is no more self-evident, in the end, than the geopolitical sovereignty of the legitimate national state. And this, in a globalized world constantly traversed by internal exiles in a closed-circuit exodus of just-in-time flows of people that some are already referring to as the migratory offensive of sustainable mobility in the twenty-first century – TRACEABILITY now being imposed on each and every one of us. This is why 'magnetic portals' have been installed in ports and airports, along with 'smart corridors' for passenger identification that are endowed with full-body scanners to strip search all those bodies in endless transit. We all know that where there's a wall there has to be a door; but the only real difference between this wall and the old fortified wall that surrounded a city is the virtual nature of the contemporary enclosure of postmodern times, as well as the clinical radiography deployed at the main entrances of our current borders.

This may help us to understand the reason behind the Sarkozy government's plan for a future 'Museum of the History of France', which would be a sort of health clinic for times past completing the one for times present, memory of which fades so quickly now, with a real danger of amnesia due to the fragile supports for the dead memories of our computers.

Then again, let's not forget that the eternal present of Einsteinian relativity is not the same as the present that ruled the day, when light was still distinct from darkness. It is the real instant, confirming what Dietrich Bonhoeffer claimed last century: 'Technology has declared war on the day.'

Contemporary with the Blitz, that verdict beautifully defines the probable translation of the 'illuminism' of the Ancients' sun worship into the 'instantaneism' of the techno-worship of the postmodern people we've all become.

We'd actually do better to swiftly abandon the grand illusion of a future 'Museum of History' and substitute, in its stead, a Ministry of the Times, a great ministry of the relativity of both the weather, *le temps qu'il fait*, and of passing time, *le temps qui passe*, time now passing so quickly. AEROPOLITICS would then cleverly complete the CHRONOPOLITICS of the time behind the GEOPOLITICAL interactivity of our real-time communications.

Thanks to such administration of duration and of the time needed, *le temps qu'il faut*, to act conscientiously and not just interact with tele-communication tools, the ecology of the weather, *le temps qu'il fait*, would take on a 'natural' intel-ligence that's currently in the process of being discriminated against, as though it were out-classed by the feats of the 'artificial' intelligence of computer programs and handy software that can do anything, and soon, undo anything . . .

Such a great ministry of Times Management would manage the vital rhythms of the weather and not just the environment; it would be a min-istry of Space Management, overseeing a space that is now exhausted not only in its biodiver-sity but also in its chrono-diversity, with seasonal shifts in climate being erased, as well as in its geo-diversity, with the differences in and extent of country landscapes being similarly erased. For, the pollution of time distances now completes the pollution of substances, water, air, fauna and flora; and the current domination of the real time of exchanges over the real space of the continents ends, as we see, in inertia. More precisely, it ends in the 'moment of inertia' of the interactive CONNECTION (*LIEN*), an instant inertia that will shortly take over from the 'fixed-property inertia' of PLACES (*LIEUX*) in a sedentariness that, all the same, goes back all the way to ancient times.

In the face of this astronomical shattering of our *emploi du temps*, our daily regimen, the shattering of a continuum that's about to go from being postmodern to become 'posthistoric', we can legitimately ask ourselves about the INTEMPORARY amnesia of technically oriented civilization. The proposed ministry of the relativity that is restricted to our incredibly cramped planet would, in fact, open up a new avenue for hope, the hope of allowing for the *kairos*, the *right moment* for action and not just interactive reaction – that future 'ghetto of CONNECTION' in a substanceless addiction that will soon supplant the 'ghetto of PLACE' of age-old sedentariness on a telluric planet that's decidedly too small for technical progress, just as it is too small for the profits of a capitalism unleashed by the systemic crash of the NANOTECHNOLOGIES of instantaneity.

It all ends, ultimately, in the 'great lockdown' of History, the unanticipated renaissance of a new form of sun worship, one requiring sacrifices that are not only *human* (sociological) but *rural* (ecological). In other words, it ends in the inevitable revival of the illuminism of light through the illuminism behind the instantaneism of light's limit speed. That is the new absolute of a god who clearly doesn't play dice, but happily dons the ridiculous cast-offs of the 'Sun King', or of Jupiter, god of the sky and of light, but also of thunder and lightning – divinity of this truly stunning, and not just explosive, instantaneity of a demandingly secular age. An age in which mono-atheism outpaces the nihilism behind the death of the gods, with the renaissance, the new age, of a late form of sun worship in which the speed of electromagnetic waves lights up, through its radiation much more than its rays, the radiant future of progressivism. This triumph of mono-atheism is particularly marked by the construction in Geneva of a circular (subterranean) cathedral, which is actually a 27 kilometre racetrack, destined to discover, at the end of the race, 'God's particle', the HADRON – at the risk of ending in the obscurantism of a 'black hole'. Such an accident in knowledge would no doubt put an end to the demand for experimental physics and thereby the exact sciences, promoting instead the eternal return of the magical thinking of the Pythagoreans of the digital and other programmers of handy software that can do anything.

So, it's all too easy to see that, with the latest electronic illuminism, transhuman societies of the animal species are metamorphosing into hybrids of the plant species as they in turn become HELIOTROPICAL and photosensitive, 'object-oriented' through the framing of point of view, and captured by the interface-to-face confrontation of the multiple screens of an environment that's suddenly gone interactive.

We might now have a better sense of the havoc wreaked by progress in a KINEMATIC energy of instantaneous transmission that has come to complete the KINETIC energy involved in the transport of bodies in the era of the industrial revolution that preceded the very recent information revolution produced by telecommunications. The kinematic energy involved in being carried away in the age of interactive synchronization rounds off the 'reality effects' produced by the kinetic energy involved in the physical movement of individuals, at high speed.

'Just-in-time-zero-stock': that slogan of large-scale commercial distribution today beautifully describes the mutation in the initial form of inertia, that of fixed-property settlement, into a final inertia, that of the instant or, more precisely, the 'moment of inertia' in the interactivity that now defines our relationship with the world. A world globalized by world time, thanks to the restrained relativity of (instantaneous) exchanges. And this relativity leads not only to Einsteinian restriction, but also to the ecosystemic reduction of the time distances of the star that carries us and supports us (with greater and greater difficulty), the original ark, EARTH, which the phenomenologist Edmund Husserl told us couldn't move, since speed is not a 'phenomenon' but the relationship between phenomena. For, the temporal compression of interactivity is equivalent to the telluric contraction of the planet of living beings: this incredibly 'Down-to-Earth' star of the QUICK, the live (*vif*), where the acceleration of the QUICK, the swift (*vite*), in the VOID (*vide*), has now become the primary issue for an ecology that is political – not transpolitical, as those pure disciples of the cult of the speed of light in the vacuum (*vide*) of deep space, the illuminists of the Last Day, would like to have us believe.

In the end, the major issue for the third millennium is indeed the issue of the regime of periodicity in an 'aeropolitics of time' that would not, all the same, negate the geopolitics of the original settling of the Earth and the CITY, that has turned into a WORLD-CITY, THE ORIGINAL ARK OF TOMORROW. Here, a metaphor springs to mind – of ocean navigation, with the invention of first the mechanical clock and then the on-board chronometer.

If the sky is indeed a monumental clock, that doesn't make it easy to decipher, despite the compass and the sextant and ASTROLABE. For, if we can calculate latitude by observing the height of stars above the horizon, longitude, on the other hand, can't be verified except by considering the time difference between two different points on the globe. That requires the use of the chronometer, whereas the 'wheelhouse hour-glass', very like a speedometer, merely showed a ship's speed, with the aid of a log, that invisible lifeline lying submerged at the end of a piece of string, graduated in knots.[1]

Surely we can't fail to see the enormous time difference that exists, today, between our at once untimely and interactive practices – practices involved in supersonic transport and instantaneous transmission – and our daily life, now so exhausted, so deprived of the intervals of time needed for reflection and responsible action. This is to say nothing of the 'casino economy', that infernal machine that is impossible to stop before a SYSTEMIC CRASH, the shipwreck of the original Ark, occurs, leading, this time, to a chaos we can well imagine . . . A Chronic UTOPIA, or a topical UCHRONIA, as some people might call the future birth of a great Ministry of the Times or, more precisely, of the weather, *le temps qu'il fait*, and the time needed, *le temps qu'il faut*, here below, in the depths of a foreclosed world. A world that would, in the end, deserve this AEROPOLITICS of the periodicity of what

1 Gilles Lapouge, *La Légende de la géographie.* Paris: Albin Michel, 2009.

is vital for chronophage societies, keen to crash, tomorrow, into the CIRCULAR time barrier at the end of the tunnel of LINEAR historicity. CERN's 'Great Hadron Collider' in Geneva has become the perfect symbol of a postmodern return of illuminism, the illuminism of the cult of light speed for a history operating in a different time zone from all common reality.

So, if we can just hang on a little while longer, the known world of our memory might well fade from the control screens of History and disappear, seemingly inadvertently.

Too Late for Private Life

> Communism hasn't disappeared, it's been privatized.
>
> Marius Oprea

Mode de vie (lifestyle) and cardiac rhythms (heart-beats), *mode de vitesse* (speed mode) and technical rhythmics (technical cycles) – that, in a nutshell, is the question posed by the TEMPO of our use of time and space in a vitality that was once run-of-the-mill but is now suffering from every-day life's electrotechnical ARHYTHMIA which never stops rocking people's consciences.

The old calendar-based systems of agrar-ian societies, their seasonal rhythms, have long yielded to the systems and rhythms of industrialization and the mass population shifts from the country to the towns. This process has, by the same token, abolished the remainder of the West's Christian rituals, with public holidays dwindling as the programmed end of lifetime employment – the practice of open-ended work contracts – spreads, along with structural unemployment. It has reached the point of pure and simple elimination of the weekly cycle now that Sunday has been subverted as a day of rest and the much-touted seven-days-a-week (7/7) made imperative.

Annual and seasonal not so long ago, weekly and daily after that, this truly historic rhythmics was to be given a fatal blow by the cybernetic information revolution. For, the acceleration of common reality swiftly makes practical life, everyday life and not just social or family life, impossible. This has recently resulted in the atomization, the sudden 'fractalization' of social units which, beyond the risks of 'communitarianism', entails the incomparably more serious risks of an emotional SYNCHRONIZATION that will lead to a 'communism of affects' on the scale of a planet reduced to nothing, where the real time of 'cyber' instantaneity will, this time, finally overtake the real space of the time differences and time distances involved in our indispensable relationship with the world. Desocialization will thereby extend people's current mental and emotional disorientation.

Media pressure already notoriously ends up exposing the private lives of select individuals, politicians, celebrities, 'top-tier' sportsmen, even of that avant-garde of progressivism, the presenters of nightly newscasts. Here, we might note, the doping of television audiences is no longer chemical but electro-optical and it has reached the point where the usual simulation of the virtual world of screens is enhanced by the rhythmical excess of a stimulation that mentally and emotionally shakes people once so attentive to the hours of the day and the months of the civil year that successfully replaced the new year of the historical calendar system and the holy year of the jubilees of yore.

One particular presenter, a woman, put it this way: 'My objective is to feel that I'm always alive, to not become mummified. But I don't know if I can keep up the pace for much longer. I know that if I'd worked less, I'd have had a second child. That will always be my great regret. But current affairs are forever wearing us down.'[1]

Presenter, male or female – this denomination is revelatory of the latest of 'futurisms': that of the electrotechnical doping perpetrated by the OMNIPRESENT instant that so relentlessly tortures former 'journalists', who've suddenly segued into 'instantaneists'. Tomorrow, it will affect each and every one of us, transforming the ordinary life of sedentarized societies, here or there, into an 'infra-ordinary' life. For, the photosensitive inertia of viewers will shortly catch up with that of their favourite presenters, the inertia of the real instant of the newsflash standing in for the fixed-property inertia of their domiciliation. The delocalization of our use of space, *l'emploi de l'espace*, will be doubled by disorientation in our use of time, *l'emploi du temps*, in a daily life once given rhythm by the alternation of days and nights, and now shattered by the breaks in rhythm caused by an entirely denatured acrobatic vitality.

It's as if the end of lifetime employment, with

1 'Audrey Pulvar enfourche une nouvelle vie', in *Paris Match*, 22 July 2009.

its very long durations and its professional con-
straints, had suddenly mutated in the face of
the disciplinary demands of the unforeseen, the
unexpected, of the 'just-in-time' nature of tight
distribution, for the very people who are already
no longer producers, actors of progress, but mere
onlookers, consumers of the background noise
of an INTERREACTIVITY that takes the place
of the INTERMEDIATION of the employees of
the not so distant past.

So, employment as a way of life, a *mode de
vie*, is superseded by life as a user's manual, *la
vie mode d'emploi*, as Georges Perec would say,
for a new kind of provisional society, one exces-
sively instrumentalized and endlessly incited to
overreact to this or that signal, all the diverse
stimuli of a permanent state of alarm. In that
state, the instantaneity of what crops up unex-
pectedly will doubtless condition the putting
into a trance not of the citizen-soldier anymore
but of a citizen-subject, within a 'social network'
that will soon replace the network based on the
physical proximity of actual people. People like
our old neighbours, who we'd so often bump
into in the PLACES behind the SOCIAL
CONNECTIVITY of our past domiciliary

inertia. The private life of each and every one of us will gradually yield to the overexposure of a semi-public life where the intimacy available to people generally will be like the intimacy enjoyed by detainees under observation in police custody. For, the old CAMERA OBSCURA of panoptical surveillance turns out to have been nothing more than a clinical symptom of the imminent obliteration of any private life.

Here, a further comment is needed. In the past, with the rule of Saint Benedict of Nursia, the sequestration of the monastic order succeeded the roaming of the wanderers of the apostate, with the Roman Church distinguishing between CONTEMPLATIVE and ACTIVE orders. Today, it would indeed seem that, for the CORELIGIONISTS of social networking, the same kind of line is being drawn between a few allegedly highly-skilled 'actives' and the anonymous mass of 'contemplatives', these Francisan friars riveted to their screens the way monks were once riveted to their breviaries, with our secular but interconnected societies once and for all sorting the sheep from the goats.

Here again, the (emotional) polar inertia that results from instantaneity and synchronization tends to supplant domiciliary inertia and the geographic localization of a social body already in a state of advanced decay where mass individualism wreaks its havoc. For, the photosensitive inertia of the mass of progress's contemplatives and the delocalization of their activities are nothing more than fatal signs of the disorientation in what Perec would call the *mode d'emploi* of their daily life.

Here, too, comparison with the religious orders is fruitful. The liturgy, 'the acts of the people', contemporary with the third millennium, revives, as though in secret, the liturgies of the people of believers. But where the Church of Christendom managed to create an equality based on Faith within a wide diversity of living conditions and spiritual riches thanks to the statics of deep-rootedness in fixed property (that of the monastery, a true laboratory of the future of our *emploi du temps*), the dynamics of the revolution in transport, and especially in computer transmissions, has abolished this form of social unity – in favour of the synchronization of common sensations. In this INTERACTIVE COMMUNISM, the real instant of audiovisual telecommunications dominates the all-too-real space of social communications, and the stand-ardization of religious beliefs and behaviours is erased thanks to the simultaneity of common feeling, with the 'community of interests' shared by all now yielding its political primacy to this community of emotion based on an individualism that is fundamentally transpolitical.

This phenomenon is further aggravated by the evolution of a culture and, swiftly afterwards, a true CULT OF EXCESS over the course of the nineteenth century and, especially, the twentieth, with the acceleration of reality itself ending in the dawn of a new form of madness, *la folie de voir*. This entails having to see at all costs – to the detriment of hearing, as well as of handling, of touch, tactility, as well as of contact.

On this score, it's time for an anecdote, the one about Richard Wagner putting his hands over his girlfriend, his lover, Malvida's eyes, while they were listening to *Tristan* and shouting at her: 'Stop looking so hard and listen!'

Ever since its Greco-Latin origins, in fact, Western philosophy has been primarily a philosophy of vision, of the various kinds of light and the forms presented to searching eyes. That has produced today's cult, this technocult of the speed of light and of the waves that convey information that has now gone MEGALOSCOPIC.

It is also what's behind the retinal persistence of an anachronistic futurism of which the NANOCHRONOLOGIES are the latest avatar. One writer has even gone so far as to claim that 'speed is the contemporary world's aristocracy' – in a nutshell, a 'racing nobility', following on from the court nobility of the Ancien Régime.

But, to get back to the European PHILOFOLLY of seeing, Westerners, and especially Latin-Europeans, like Latin-Americans, need public passions. After the great passion of triumphant Christianity, it seems they opted for the great passion of a Progress that was to end, last century, in the very brief passion for speeding up the history of the twentieth century. The limit speed of waves then stole a march on the wealth of nations, whose end, whose defeat, 'Communism' was supposed to mark, thanks to the cosmism of escape velocity that enabled escape from terrestrial gravity – first by Sputnik, then by the MIR station that signalled that cosmism's failure and disappearance. The TURBOCAPITALISM of the Single Market then took over in the age of international economic integration thanks to the very latest 'escape velocity', residing within the domain of cybernetics and anticipating the deliverance, this time in the name of ecology, of a humanity polluted by discovery of a habitable EXOPLANET, free-market COSMOTHEISM thereby following hot on the heels of the social COSMISM of the old Soviet Empire.

In fact, it has only ever been one small step from the mass portable empire to the otherworld exodus of populations – 'one small step for man but a giant leap for mankind', as Neil Armstrong once said, as he disembarked on the night star – a star or, more precisely, a nightspot, that some would now like to see back on the agenda, despite President Obama's rejection of the idea.

One thing's for sure and that is that it's now too late to have a private life. Yesterday's 'solitary' crowds, who we're told are now so 'smart', are nothing more than hordes primed for a long-haul exodus, OUT-OF-THIS-WORLD exile beyond our earthly homeland, for the liberated and dispersed societies of the great diaspora, deportation having been merely a fatal sign of an EXTERNALIZATION that has no future, where movement is all and the goal is pointless.

Nowadays, unlike in the industrial era of manufacturing plants and factories analysed by Marxism, we no longer explore – we expel. We also exterminate more and more frequently, the STOP EJECT of those damned to exodus thereby taking over from the STAND BY of yore!

Both the settling of the peasantry on the land where it all began and the fixed-property inertia of the city-dweller are now being overtaken by the real instant's devastating inertia or, more precisely, its moment of inertia, in an INTERACTIVE simultaneity that shakes up all settling down, any deep rootedness. On that score, note that the very first law of urbanism is: retention of the site. At this stage in the history of human, but also urban, settlement, 'territorial insecurity' is at an all-time high and the territorial sovereignty of the legitimate national state is in danger of being lost forever in the face of the HYPERCOLONIALIST threat posed by sovereign wealth funds' grubby land-grabbing, monopolizing all lands and their resources. The old politics of the *droit du sol*, the right to citizenship, gives way all of a sudden in the face of the exorbitant privileges of a sort of AEROPOLITICS, which is not only ecological but economic. This is what lies behind the *droit du ciel*, the right to the sky, to heaven, to all the heavens and to the virtual space of interconnected financial markets, with the high-frequency traders who engage in flash trading here playing Russian roulette, every day, with the fate of the world in a lightning war whose weaponry is provided by high-flying (*sic*) cybernetic systems, the old sovereignty of nations gradually disappearing. What shoots to the fore instead is a META-GEOPHYSICAL politics for nations that are 'stateless', or as good as, now that the correligionists of humanity's SERVOMOTOR are joining forces with those of a computerized PANTHEISM. Gaia, the Earth Goddess of triumphant ecology, is already a symptom of this.

With the revolution in the financial industry and its mathematical models leading to the systemic chaos we're all only too familiar with and, in this age of an anthropocentrism that is wreaking havoc with our climates and causing whole peoples to go into exodus, we actually have no choice but to look long and hard at the structural energy of an anthropodynamics of the history of humanity in which territorial identity is in danger of shortly being lost altogether, now that we're seeing the beginnings of a sort of instant traceability of the social body as well as of each of its members.

If the aerostatic form of sedentary human settlement was once geographically indexed, the aerodynamic form of exclusion, and of the *expelled* that now prevails over of the *exploited* of full employment, is not indexed at all.

Hidden behind freedom of movement and mass tourism, the HABITABLE CIRCULATION involved in the forced exile of both the 'internally displaced persons' of African states and the 'delocalized persons' of developed countries merits more than just a cartography now. It merits a constantly updated trajectography – a sort of PLANETARIUM of the flows of populations in permanent transit – if we are to attempt to trace this uncivilized choreography of the excluded, whose mortality rates never cease growing, beyond the chaos in moral values, to the point of extermination and genocide.

Here, a further comment springs to mind. If the political engagement of the responsible individual not long ago joined forces with the brand of engagement promoted by Sartrian existentialism, we have to say that, in this era of mass individualism of a COMMUNISM OF AFFECTS that are synchronized, what prevails is being carried away, *l'emportement*. This, in both the literal and metaphorical senses of the term: as in the mobile and the portable, and in loss of self-control. The acceleration of reality is now part and parcel of the loss of all self-control, when even the accelerating history of historical materialism still took its time – the time needed to get a sense of past history as well as the time involved in a radiant future that Soviet cosmism would try to get off the ground again once the USSR collapsed.

In this sense, the COSMOTHEISM that is once again rampant in the West, in tandem with ecology and the desperate quest for an exoplanetary refuge, takes us back to the astronautical hallucinations that so cleverly masked the evident failure of 'progress' in the era of the balance of atomic terror between the great Eastern and Western blocs.

By way of confirmation, we might point out that, at the end of July 2009, the very first 'International Extraterrestrial Summit' took place in Barcelona. This was followed at the end of August that same year by a beefed-up edition of Operation Suricate, designed to track the trajectories of UFOs all over Europe, thanks to hundreds of telescopes trained on the firmament, in a bid to correlate sightings.

Speaking of the contemplative nature of contemporary man, a journalist jokingly put it this way: 'He's an exhibitionist who's been placed under observation in custody.'

Surrounded by his screens and subject to video control and the discipline of programs, as well as to the rules of interactivity, this new PHOTOSENSITIVE being turns into a consenting victim of a progress that amputates his private life, with electro-optical addiction to information more and more alienating him from his sense of self.

Hence the denial of engagement per se (political, syndicalist . . .) in favour of an *emportement* – getting carried away, rage – that only mass individualism has the knack of, where once collectivism merely imposed engagement, the fact of having only one party facilitating the lack of any 'conscientious objection'!

The inertia of the photosensitive onlooker thus corresponds to the mutation of the traveller and the furtive gliding of a mode of private 'auto-mobile' transport, that mode of public transport involved in the mass exodus of interconnected individualities.

With naval or aeronautical BULK CARRIERS, *GROS PORTEURS*, or, better still, *MÈRES PORTEUSES*, surrogate mothers carrying out gestation for others, the constant expansion of the carrying capacity of our various vehicles does indeed flag the sudden shift in travel, which was solitary not so long ago but will soon be embarked on (embedded) communally as we head to uncertain destinations where speed becomes a kind of destiny.

Here, we might note a new type of highly manoeuvrable transport plane that is particularly revelatory of the coming revolution in haulage. The SKYLANDER, manufactured in France, is a veritable LANDROVER of the sky, capable of operating in difficult conditions and hostile environments, with maximum payloads and flight ranges. Canada's TWIN OTTER, said to be a 'rustic aircraft', is also a versatile twin-engine turboprop that can take on freight or passengers as required in conditions of rudimentary comfort, where passengers travel standing up, like cattle in a cattle truck, while awaiting further, even more radical, developments.

But let's get back to the case of the 'surrogate mother', so brilliantly analysed by the French philosopher Sylviane Agacinski. This *living tool*, this metabolical vehicle, 'trivializes pregnancy, which is reduced to simple foetal transport, certain women now even being seen as akin to chartered planes that can effect a sort of co-cartage for others'.[1]

These are all so many panicky signs of the imminent end of a private life deprived of all 'filial' identity, from birth on; and when we come of age, we can expect to see ourselves deprived also of any 'territorial' identity, *in situ*, by the biopolitical requirement of unending 'social' traceability. The imperatives of ecological security in this latest *LEBENSRAUM* will also necessitate the same control over distribution to the detriment of stocks and of the historical accumulation of civil law and the 'rights of man' that still, until recently, prevailed. This is why we're seeing the gradual disappearance of self-control and the medical evacuation, by airlift, of the old

1 Sylviane Agacinski, *Corps en miettes*. Paris: Flammarion, 2009.

way of life, with its customary urbanity following on from peasant life, that life lived from day to day, to the rhythm of the seasons, in a way the nanochronological acceleration of the interactive instant no longer allows.

Over the course of the 1920s, writer Joseph Roth sensed the deeper significance of the style of architecture known as 'the international style', in which the culling of ornament, as well as of volumes, came with the hygienist myth of maximum sunlight and transparency for housing. The SHOP WINDOW was poised to be raised into a GLASS BUILDING, causing all intimacy to be lost to inhabitants overexposed to the eyes of all, the loss of the temporal bearings of daily life being accompanied by a disorientation in the rhythms of life. The lighting of towns, at night, was to be further rounded off by the elimination of load-bearing walls, with the 'curtain wall' and automatic blinds serving as shutters for the 'cameras lucidas' of an era in which the snapshot would shortly overcome the hold of long-term durations and the purely promotional MEDIA BUILDING would even illuminate the public space of the city, as in Times Square.

Within this same order of ideas of a coming 'post-intimacy', we might note how joint tenancy is gradually turning into a mode of coexistence these days. For often quite different reasons, then, we are seeing the revival of the Soviet utopia of the 'communal household' and the shared apartment – these so-called SOCIAL CONDENSERS for which the futurist architect, Melnikov, provided the theory.

Through economic necessity, given the costs of renting, people now boast on the Internet of the concept of a 'unit of collective life', as the Partage-Senior (Sharing for Seniors) Association indicates: 'A mixed nest of four or five people and what you get is quite a different ambiance where joint tenants feel freer.'

A woman who runs a similar association goes as far as telling journalists that: 'Joint tenancy is the world's best anti-depressant.'

Other organizations go even further in this disorientation of the old way of life, offering a 'life plan aboard a sailing ship' tailored to seniors who might fancy an open-ended trip around the world . . . Between container ships, where illegal immigrants stow away at the risk of their lives, and these luxury cruises for tourists of desolation, who fritter away the inheritance so they can live permanently on an ocean liner since that turns out to be less expensive in the end than a decent retirement home, there is all the difference in the world – the difference between the headlong flight of the desperate and sheer ambulatory madness.

In the same category of gyration as that performed by the GYROWAVES of exodus, these new wandering monks of no fixed abode, we might cite an eccentric practice that typifies the new form of travel for people in endless transit. Couch surfing is a mode of hospitality that consists in offering free accommodation in your own home to travellers met over the Internet. With these joint tenants for a night, the guest room turns into a room in a guest house for strangers.

To travel, to comb the world without having to part with any cash thanks to hitch-hiking and some couch-surfer network – that was the aim of an idealist initiative launched in 1949, after the Second World War, by Gary Davis, that apostle of a globalized citizenship which has today been cunningly diverted from its peaceful objectives.

Hotelier or Hospitaller of the Net? With couch-surfing, the blurring of genres is clear. Intimacy, once sought out of a sense of propriety, seems to be mistaken for concealment, as though of some shameful disease . . .

All this reproduces fairly faithfully the excesses of telesurveillance, initially limited to the space of streets and other places of transit, then introduced into the common parts of buildings, car parks or entrance halls.

Here again, the transparency of public space followed by private spaces leads to the transappearance of the intercom, or security phone, and its camera.

Another example of this is the recent growth in the MEGALOSCOPY of Google Earth, with its research engine, Google Maps, aiming to visualize the entire world. Following the use of observation satellites, the firm is developing Google Street, using a specialized car in street-by-street reconnaissance of cities – and setting off a whole debate on respect for private life in doing so. In the face of resistance at local council level, Google decided to launch Street View, using bicycles that are each equipped with a GPS and cameras to film France and other countries. Their incredibly diverse landscapes will then be digitized to feed Google's giant mapping project.

Why don't we take this deadly OVER-EXPOSURE of private life that is now spreading as far as the eye can see just a little bit further? Imagine that, following on from the fixed cameras set up at major intersections to ensure road traffic safety or at the entrances to buildings to ensure security, couch surfing is already taking us to the next, the ultimate, level of revelation. This is where the Google Home inspector turns up on your doorstep, covered in portable cameras designed to reveal to all and sundry the level of comfort of the bathrooms on offer to low-budget tourists benefitting from the hospitality of the Internet's social networks!

'The acceleration of History is disturbing. We're forced to call ourselves into question much more routinely than in the past. [. . .] The shifting present causes great anxiety. Our sense of the everyday is swept away by a feeling of inevitability. That feeling amounts to a kind of collective depression.' So said Nathalie Kosciusko-Morizet, France's then Secretary of State for Strategic Planning, in the summer of 2009. But talking of 'depression' isn't saying much. Wherever acceleration of the reality of the moment prevails over acceleration of the history of the famous 'shifting present', what is called into question, at every instant, is the real presence of people and things that, only yesterday, seemed to lastingly surround us. As an elderly friend, whose young wife never stopped travelling, sadly confessed to me once: 'She doesn't travel to forget she's just used to not seeing me anymore.'

With the exodus of societies that have once again become dispersed, travel is a form of widowhood or widowerhood that encourages each and every one of us to no longer see what once tied us to, rooted us in, a common past, country, neighbourhood, neighbours, family or spouse. This is also what the end of private life is, this endless translation of the intimacy of the sedentary homebody into the *extimacy* of transportation whereby the traveller is not so much a new nomad as a passenger in the middle of getting a divorce, carried away by the inevitability of everyday exile . . .

To try to facilitate reconciliation proceedings, a company in Brussels called Fasten Seat Belts airs on airport screens a series of video clips in twenty languages. The clips are designed to make 'good manners' easier to achieve in foreign countries, with just a few key phrases . . . As the woman in charge of the project points out: 'It's funny, people are travelling more and more, but some of them behave exactly as they do at home. They're always in shorts and thongs and only speak their native language.'[1]

No one really travels; in fact, they flee, they escape a hated, stressful daily grind. The old HOME OF ONE'S OWN is now ON ONE, in the panoply of communicating objects, electronic trinkets, that you carry away with you, in this amicable divorce of repeat delocalization.

Is this due to the increase in life expectancy? We might note, whatever the case may be, that the divorce rate for people sixty years and older has risen by close to 30% for women and 40% for men. Also according to France's *Institut nationale d'études démographiques* (INED), it's worse for people in their fifties, as the rates have practically doubled.

Here again, we notice the same acceleration as with public transport: for some, it's a case of supersonic and shortly hypersupersonic flight; for others, express divorce. Since 45% of marriages now end in divorce, we may as well simplify

1 *Le Monde*, 16 August 2009.

the usual procedure straight away and make the break of load between spouses even faster and cheaper with a law that specifically combats the inertia of husbands and wives, low-cost divorce trivializing the family saga of yore. That's why Rachida Dati's last project, as Keeper of the Seals and Minister of Justice, was to reform divorce so that a couple can now separate, *subito presto*, simply by coming before their notary.[1]

All of this makes it feel as though, by endlessly shrinking – like the times involved in the 'turnover rate' from moving in to moving out – marriage is starting to last about as long as what occurs in 'play-acting', the 'edutainment' practice that is now nothing more than the staging of the contemporary loss of all sense of reality in this age of telecommunications and the instant delocalization they trigger.

Addiction to constant travel, like addiction to changing partners, is now part of the illusory nature of the autonomy of the old way of life, the fashion for coaches taking over from the fashion for the spiritual advisers of religious orders or the master thinkers of totalitarian militantism.

1 *Libération*, 18 August 2009.

A striking example of this shift in communal sedentariness can be seen, right now, in the impact of the Internet on monastic life, particularly in women's convents where, to date, only 25 of France's surviving 270 monasteries are still resistant to using the WEB – despite 'the underhand imposition of a new pace of communication that is slipping into the spirit of monastic time', as a Cistercian monk from Hauterive points out.[1]

Yet everyone insists on the essential discrimination of each monk: 'The material enclosure is not an absolute; it is a means. The main question is rather: how to experience the relationship to the world (to the whole world instantaneously). The Internet forces us to have another look at our borders and to internalize that enclosure.'[2]

The WEB, in fact, potentially opens all the doors and steps through all the gates of the monastic enclosure. Which is why the Benedictines of Bec-Hellouin Abbey took the initiative of organizing a session on the subject in the autumn of 2009.

As Dom Notker Wolf, primate of the order,

1 *La Croix*, 7 October 2009.
2 *Ibid.*

noted: 'Detachment, silence and solitude, or else: the culture of CONNECTION and EVERYTHING, NOW. There is no more space to wait in, no more space in which to desire the infinite. In this culture, waiting is always negative. ... It means waiting for the end of an operation and not for an encounter.' Apropos the contemplative life of the convent, he concludes: 'We shouldn't so much regulate things based on virtual culture, but on monastic culture.'[1]

It's pointless to add here that the sedentariness of this spiritual culture matches, in all respects, the sedentariness behind the customary urbanity of the city and of the fixed settlement of populations that were once nomadi, like the monks of earlier orders – the rule of Saint Benedict. Those monks were also nomadic (*gyrovague*) and subject to unforeseen events in a meandering that was conducive to all kinds of deviant behaviour, contemplation for them being just a solitary form of prayer.

Lastly, we might mention that, once he was back from the concentration camps, Primo Levi would spend hours in front of his computer

1 *Ibid.*

screen without writing, or at his mother's bedside, waiting for night and the release of sleep, telling his friends and family over and over again, before throwing himself down the stairwell of his home and killing himself: 'This is worse than at Auschwitz.'[1]

The end of private life is a new kind of poverty in terms of 'living conditions' and not just 'the cost of living' anymore. The contemporary drop in social standing implied by the emergence of a community of synchronized emotions turns into a disaffiliation at once both familial and social that will eventually go 'national' and finally 'territorial', with the undermining of the PLACE as well as the CONNECTION of common life. Right now we are seeing the first signs of a disaffiliation that is animal, with the blurring of MASCULINE and FEMININE genders inaugurating an imminent DEMATERNALIZATION of women. No doubt that will end, tomorrow, in the disconnection of reproduction from the human race, a future 'post-sexuality' that will

1 Ernesto Ferrero, *Primo Levi. L'écrivain au microscope*. Paris: Liana Levi, 2009.

supposedly be so liberating for women as well
as for their incredibly cumbersome pregnancy.
The industrialization of life will then take over
where the industrialization of death left off, in the
camps where one Dr Mengele reigned supreme,
incredibly preoccupied as he was with twin births
and cloning.

In fact, the notion of a crime against humanity,
elaborated nearly a century ago, no longer exclu-
sively concerns the extermination of all or part of
the human race – along the lines of the clinical
genocide perpetrated by the Nazis, or even the
atomic *geocide* of the Cold War period, with its
balance of terror. It more simply concerns the
ultimate endangering of our daily routines, of a
'way of life' that was, in the end, quite ordinary. In
the near future, if we're not careful, this will lead
to a vitality made fundamentally uninhabitable
by the excessiveness of an oppressive eagerness,
a life without a 'user's manual', in the words of
Georges Perec, an INFRA-ORDINARY vivacity
– until biodiversity of the human kind is finally
exhausted.

To illustrate this probable DISLOCATION
in daily life, we might cite a case brought before
the industrial tribunal of Oyonnax, a town in the

Ain region of France. In 2009, the tribunal had to examine a complaint 'for a violation of the right to a family life' brought by the employees of the ED supermarket, fired for refusing to work on Sundays, failure to observe working hours and insubordination. Their lawyer put it this way: 'Since there is no case law dealing with working on Sundays, we'll base our case on a ruling of the final Court of Appeal which says that, for night work, the salaried employee needs to have signed an agreement.' She concludes, 'It will actually be particularly interesting to see if the industrial tribunal recognizes the RIGHT TO A FAMILY LIFE as a higher principle than the right to paid work.'[1]

Day and night, all through the week and on Sundays, twenty-four hours a day, seven days a week . . . that's a way of life that has no directions for use, no *mode d'emploi*, other than the repetition of repetitive processes. After the forced localization of the age of de-industrialization, forced dislocation is getting under way to the rhythm of a Progress now openly unnatural. Meanwhile, the case would seem tricky to

1 *La Croix*, 16 October 2009.

plead as the 'right to refuse', to 'civil conscientious objection', has scarcely any reality as a legal entity.

Being suicidal was once a psychological state, but it can consequently turn sociological, when we deregulate the way we regulate time and its rhythms, their *mode d'emploi*, to the point of causing anxiety, the permanent anguish of communities, as is already happening in telecommunications companies where the harm done by stress has become fatal.

'We must insist that the future does not belong to fear', President Obama told the United Nations in his address of September 2009. He was talking about the major risks of nuclear proliferation. But, more intimately, this statement should also apply to the issue of our *mode de vie*, our way of life, the everyday life of a period marked by precariousness and the instability of the TEMPO driving local communities in the grip of the fear caused by the devastating progress in interactive technology. That progress is nothing more than the progress of a deliriously bustling eagerness, not to say a collective rage, triggered by a sudden panic that's turned into a PANDEMIC. A pandemic that has everything to do with the reality effect of acceleration of information and its sudden demands. For, the INSTANTANEITY of the disarray of each one of us will soon contaminate the way of life of all.

So, after the rise of MILITARY DETER-RENCE and its fall at the end of the cold war, it would seem that the 'cold panic' of a world overexposed to major risks is beginning to be felt. These risks include not only blind terrorism but also ecology and, especially, a tyrannical political economics, with the temptation, for certain fans of 'personal space', of launching what would this time amount to CIVIL DETERRENCE. The governance of public fear would then shift from the battlefield of the past to the marketplace. In other words, to an everyday life that will soon be made impossible, ravaged as it is by the 'domestic terror' of each and every instant; the excess speed of the clashing tasks to be performed taking over from the crashes once involved in road accidents.

Isn't there already talk, here and there, of the future requirements for a SUSTAINABLE MOBILITY that will best ensure sustainable development? Big fans of management through stress, certain CEOs even claim that 'we can no longer let immobility set in', suggesting that the 'TIME TO MOVE' doctrine should be imposed throughout the globalized business firm. Everywhere you look, the 'broadband' of telecommunications is contaminating the use to which we put the week, its *mode d'emploi*, with the elimination of Sunday as a day-off followed by the elimination of the daily interruption of lunch. Imposition of the JUST-IN-TIME continuous day anticipates the inertia of the fatal instant and the unstoppable offensive of the NANOCHRONOLOGIES, along the lines of the 'lightning crash' of 6 May 2010, when the wall of Wall Street suddenly crashed into the wall of money, the MONEY BARRIER, at precisely 2.25 pm.

After the continuum (of terrestrial spacetime), till now seen as the *adjustment variable* of our various activities, the dromospheric pressure of technical progress now affects individuality throughout the whole panoply of populations subject to the death throes of instantaneous interactivity. For, this latest tyranny suddenly becomes the *ultimate variable* in a demographic adjustment of profit. The *quantitative* Malthusianism of the past is now coupled with a *qualitative* Malthusianism, whereby the usual ethnic racism will be rounded off by an 'Olympic' racism. Sports competitions and the feats of the latest 'stadium gods' will then abandon the podium for an on-the-spot race, opting for the inertia of those that telecommunications have locked up alive – in other words, the victims of electronic doping: the doping carried out by the cybernetic futurism of the global governance of humanity.

This is the reason for the successive disaffiliations mentioned above, with the probable decline in politics and the geopolitics of place as well as of social connection, *in situ* and *hic et nunc*, in favour of simultaneity and its teleobjective ubiquity. It is also the reason for the 'progressive' externalization of connections of all kinds and the repetitive delocalization of common space and public services – in other words of the democratic city, as we learned about it through the history of settlement.

And so, after the disintegration of matter through nuclear fission, we are now looking on, powerless or as good as, at the early stages of the disintegration of the historical transition of past time and at the fusion/confusion of the shareholder in this COMMUNION OF THE SAINTS of interactivity's global brain. The social body suddenly metamorphoses into a sort of mystical body of humanity perfected, with the DROMOSPHERE of acceleration standing in, *in extremis*, for the NOOSPHERE, the sphere of human thought of God's elect, according to Teilhard de Chardin, himself a victim of the great 'brainwashing' of the propaganda of Progress.

The Great Accelerator

Arrival of old, you will go everywhere.
Rimbaud, 'To a Reason'

Circuit, short-circuit – there is no circus without a circle, the *kuklos* of Ancient Greece and the Olympic cyclades of the acceleration of old! In 2009, a year after the launch, in the middle of the economic crisis, of the Great Accelerator, that CATHEDRAL built by CERN in Geneva, a circular TEMPLE built for the last lap of the Formula 1 world championship opened in Abu Dhabi – that is, in the middle of the desert.

Speed of light for the fans of physics and of the HADRON, the particle known as 'God's particle' and sought in vain even then, CERN's

collider having broken down . . . *Light of speed* for
the designers of the Abu Dhabi racetrack according to whom 'this circuit is the only one in the
world designed so spectators have a full view', the
DROMOLOGICAL prowess so vainly sought
by the physicists of the infinitely small was coupled here – one year later – with a prowess that
is DROMOSCOPIC, by supporters of the infinitely big of the spectacle of acceleration. This, at
a time when the automobile was being 'scrapped',
in France, in a bid to restart an industry that's in
the doldrums . . .

'If time is money, you might as well gain both!'
This slogan of a low-budget airline company
couldn't better describe the current state of mind
for addicts of a great financial casino, which is
itself in crisis. On 11 June 2010, it imposed on
Wall Street a CIRCUIT-BREAKER system for
the markets of high-frequency flash trading, In
a bid to avoid a repetition of the lightning crash
that threw the stock exchange into a spin on 6
May 2010, at precisely 2.25 pm.

After General Motors went bankrupt, Toyota
Motors was so badly shaken by the crisis that
it announced its immediate withdrawal from
Formula 1 racing and gave up hosting Japan's

2010 Grand Prix, at its Mount Fuji circuit, in order to commit itself to finding fresh solutions to the problems of domestic mobility.

This is what a special correspondent from the newspaper, *Le Figaro*, had to say about the 'Tokyo Motor Show':

'I'd never tested a new model on a showroom carpet before. Yet it was on the eighth floor of an office block that I was initiated into the future of driving in an iREAL; this single-seater vehicle certainly makes do with very little room [*sic*], the equivalent of a comfortable armchair mounted on three wheels.'[1]

If the Japanese motor company is having trouble attracting younger generations to the car, it is now effectively launching itself into the more restrained mobility of adults and especially seniors. Being longstanding consumers of domestic automobility already, why wouldn't seniors turn out to be tomorrow's great fans of 'these electric single-seaters that can go on the footpath, if not inside an apartment building and even take the lift'?[2]

1 *Le Figaro*, 30 October 2009.
2 *Ibid.*

Hence the invention of this orthopaedic pros-
thesis aimed at the seniors market, a market that
will, tomorrow, explode throughout the indus-
trialized world. That prospect for growth will
be part and parcel of a vogue in stacks of very
high buildings, these TOWERS that are already
poking up in the tens of thousands in Japanese and
Chinese cities, such as Chongqing, with its thirty
million inhabitants. Nicknamed FOG CITY,
Chongqing is one of the most polluted cities on
the planet. These days its centre is cluttered with
hundreds of wrecks of abandoned taxis.

Dreaded by men in perfect health, with the
so aptly named iReal, the wheelchair for crip-
ples turns into a somewhat fatal solution to the
wreck of the city to come and to the failure of
tomorrow's concentration camp-like world city.

With the recent promotion of this mis-
identified travelling object, the fundamentally
INCAPACITATING nature of the technical progress behind this 'piece of furniture on
wheels' is obvious and echoes the biblical fables
of the blind man and the paralytic.

The iReal engine is actually driven by hand,
thanks to two buttons like the ones used in video
games: 'No reverse, you just turn hard left or

right and swivel round on the spot. It's as simple as a video-game console and requires only small movements of the right or left wrist. As for speed, that's limited to 6 km an hour, but a rapid-speed setting of up to 30 km an hour is available!'[1]

We are, obviously, far here from the straight line of the Abu Dhabi speedway on which single-seaters travel at over 300 km an hour. But we're every bit as far, it would seem, from the 100 m world record of Usain Bolt who, with his own two legs, ran at over 37 km an hour on average around the Berlin stadium track during the world athletic championships on 15 August 2009 – the 'feast of the Assumption'!

If not exactly rising up into the sky, the stadium god here is like the Hermes of myth, that god of travellers but also of thieves, cheats, the issue of doping remaining today unresolved for the whole array of sports feats in these days of the paralympic exploits of genetic engineering of GMOs.

Where André Gorz once condemned INCAPACITATING occupations as being likely to lead to automation and a structural unemploy-

---

1 *Le Figaro*, 30 October 2009.

ment that would be final and no longer cyclical, we note that it's now the 'progressives' of all stripes that are accusing galloping automation of crimes against humanity. Such widespread automation no longer leads to anything but inertia, the paralysis brought on by a so-called improvement in productivity whereby the human body tends to lose, one by one, the characteristics of the ANIMAL realm that once distinguished man from plant and mineral!

'It's our souls we need to change, not the climate', prescribed Seneca, that apostle of an ecology of the moving being, this living being whose *anima* is obviously not a 'genus', as sex is for some people, but a realm – the realm of a species endowed with the movement of being, where 'marriage is when you espouse travel'[1] . . . especially when the latter is circular!

In fact, the historic expansion of the accelerating sphere of our physical activities – once so rich in experiences, with the language of dance and the choreography of voyages of initiation in which we set out to discover the vastness of our own world – today leads to the law of least

1 A Canadian proverb.

action of cybernetic interactivity. In other words, to the 'moment of inertia' of instantaneous interaction and, so, to postural disability, the unseen loss of the first of our freedoms, the freedom of movement that characterized the human race.

So, anticipating the development of the NANOTECHNOLOGIES of the infinitely small of 'progress', but also the development of the NANOCHRONOLOGIES of the infinitely short-term of cybernetic instantaneity – in other words, the definitive powerlessness of our awareness of the facts and of our judgement of values in the face of the sudden metamorphosis of our environment – we still have to figure out the actual nature of our responsibility regarding the 'pollution' caused by technological progress, as well as by the exhaustion of the chrono-diversity of the instant, an instant from now on not so much present as absent from our awareness of our behaviours.

Just after attempting to commit suicide, Catherine Kokoszka, the head of the Paris department of legal protection of minors, wrote:

'Anything that goes too fast drives you insane, destroys you. I almost died because I spent my life at my job, quite convinced I was upholding the educational values of the institution. I almost died of the deafness of an institution that didn't understand that everything was going too fast, so fast we could no longer keep up [. . .] and that the acceleration of change was undermining the institution's educational mission and producing abuse. The infernal machine presses on, alas, without worrying about human beings.'[1]

Incapacitating occupation yesterday, abusive administration today. Tomorrow, what will happen when the CYBERWORLD has once and for all subverted the space and time, the continuum, of our fate? Yet no one is worrying about that particular tsunami, or about the dromospheric pressure already overwhelming populations in distress. People are merely being sensitized to the dangers of atmospheric pressure, of climate change, of a thoroughly contaminated world. No one is ever concerned about being locked up behind the closed doors of the cyclotron of cybernetics.

In an important report on stress at work handed to the French government in the autumn of

1 *Le Monde*, 5 November 2009.

2009, we learned that 33% of salaried employees are now scared at work. In this statistical stocktake of psychological and social risks, we also learned that for 22.6% of staff it is the quantity of work that is too often excessive, whereas for 30% it is the quality itself of the work that is at issue, since the pressure of time no longer gives people enough time to finish what they're doing.[1]

Once upon a time, people were familiar in advance with the fear of forced labour in penal colonies to which convicts, *forçats*, were deported. But what dominates in the middle of these liberal times is fear of chosen work – no matter what the nature of the job or the task at hand.

The other characteristic of this enquiry shows that 42% of salaried employees feel, as unbearable stress, the obligation to hide their emotions while they're at work, an obligation written into their contract.

We see, then, that this psychopathological approach to jobs, already threatened on all sides with being moved off-shore or with the productivity gains of all-out automation, has incapacitating and abusive dimensions that reinforce each other

1 *Sud-Ouest*, October 2009.

– mutually – to the point where progress, which, to Edgar Allan Poe, in the nineteenth century, was just the heresy of decrepitude, has suddenly, in the twenty-first century, turned into the frenzy of stupefaction.

Thanks to the rise of technology and its tools, science has in fact become not only functional but also, above all, functionalist . . . since function now generates the component!

Today the most insignificant of technological pseudo-innovations very quickly becomes a 'hi-tech industry', and then a system for creating panic, as we've seen with the WEB and its all-encompassing network, without any precautions being taken in their use. This will soon lead to the great breakdown of the Internet, the explosion of the information bomb, which will probably do irreparable damage to the digital economy.[1]

Apropos, note the current craze for nanotechnologies that nothing will now stop, any more than the bio-engineering of GMOs was stopped yesterday, or geo-engineering of the climate will be stopped tomorrow, or not long after.

1 Paul Virilio, *The Information Bomb*, tr. Chris Turner. London: Verso, 2005.

The latest confirmation of this is the setting up, in Beijing, of a Bureau of Meteorological Modifications, responsible for the national climate of China. As it happens, the bureau recently weathered an avalanche of criticism for having induced unseasonal snowfalls. Those snowfalls grounded hundreds of planes and caused a number of road accidents for Beijing residents caught out by a phenomenon created by the mass dispersion of chemical products in clouds in a bid to relieve the persistent drought in the north of the country.[1]

But the fatal convergence, noted in the pages above, of control and abuse in the workplace, can also be explained by the fact that in China, as elsewhere, it is the diverse forms of the TOTALITARIAN experience that are in turn converging. The globalization of the Single Market and the instantaneity of interactive telecommunications are inducing a fusion/confusion of extremisms and the deliberate hybridization of this 'tyranny of real time', this COSMOTHEISM, behind a turbocapitalism that reproduces the excesses of Soviet COSMISM in the days just

1 *Sud-Ouest*, October 2009.

before the USSR imploded – the big bang of historical materialism ending in the very cybernetic accident of which we are now victims. The SYSTEMIC CRASH of Wall Street illustrates perfectly not only the Gargantuan nature of a 'science without a conscience' which is nothing more than the 'ruin of the soul'. Above all, it exposes the Gargantuan appetite of an economic science that is now without confidence, being nothing more than the 'ruin of the Single Market', the very possibility of turboprofit through high-frequency trading suddenly coming to an end, or close to it, for one very simple reason: confidence is one thing that can never be instant!

That is the reason for this unsayable fear of stock market volatility in the face of the BIG CRUNCH of credit – in other words, of investors' belief and speculative faith when confronted by the extreme uncertainty of the moment. In May 2010, that fear lead to what traders themselves call 'the fear index', the Market Volatility Index (MVI). This barometer of anticipated market volatility was conceived as early as 1993, while the CRASH of 19 October 1987 was still fresh in everyone's mind.

This is where the most crucial question comes

in: has INSTANTANEITY become, for the materialists of the Single Market, what ETERNITY once was for the spiritualists?

With the development of money in the Middle Ages, the time also came for serious debate about the legitimacy of credit and of interest-bearing loans. Usury was prohibited for Christians and considered a mortal sin, an act of theft, theft of time, which belongs only to God, since 'interest charges the time that has elapsed between the loan and its reimbursement'.[1]

Today we can easily imagine how this issue might once again call into question the relativity of time, of spacetime and its continuum, which is at the centre of the debates on the future of tomorrow's world economy.

If this were indeed the case, the futurism of the instant would make its entry both in THEOLOGY and in the ETHOLOGY of the stock exchange of values, with the political economics of speed merging, from then on, with that of the wealth of nations.

Meanwhile, an event way outside the norm

1 Jacques Le Goff, *Le Moyen Âge et l'argent*. Paris: Perrin, 2010.

occurred at precisely 2.25 pm on 6 May 2010. This was a FLASH CRASH, in which the Dow Jones plummeted a thousand points in just a few minutes. For the American Stock Exchange watchdog, the Securities and Exchange Commission (SEC), which discounted all proof of human error, computer hacking or cybernetic terrorist attack, this catastrophic event urgently imposed the putting in place of harmonized and above all synchronized circuit-breakers on a scale covering the entire market. This was done, as early as 11 June, for the electronic trading platforms of Wall Street.

So, after the MONEY WALL produced by the accumulation of capital, Mary Schapiro, the chair of the Securities and Exchange Commission in New York, put up another kind of 'dividing wall', a TIME BARRIER against cybernetic acceleration of felonies (insider trading in the finance sector or terrorist attacks by hackers . . .). But that move begs a supremely important strategic question, one that is undecidable: 'When you are incapable of detecting the origin of a stock exchange crash and, so, find it impossible to know if it's a CYBER ATTACK of some reach by one state against another, or whether it's a SYSTEMIC CRASH that's purely accidental, what do you do?'

'We need to forget about time at the most fundamental level. We don't need that particular parameter to describe the world that surrounds us. The theoretical framework I propose allows us to do without it: this is the framework of loop quantum gravity.' So speaks the physicist Carlo Rovelli, an adept, like so many others, at the confusion of the general relativity of the physics of the infinitely big and the quantum mechanics of the infinitely small.

After the *End of History* was forecast last century, the *End of Time* is now being forecast, certainly in theoretical physics, but also in relation to political economics.

In the end, what is most revealing in this general disarray is perhaps what Benoit Mandelbrot claimed in 2004, when he said that the conventional mathematical models employed by the stock market 'are not only wrong; they are dangerously wrong.'[1]

1 Benoit Mandelbrot, *The (Mis)Behaviour of Markets*. New York: Basic Books, 2004, p. 276.

Faced with the repetition of a crash that will soon be systemic, we have no choice but to ask ourselves about the powerlessness of savvy economists to interpret the alarm bells that have been ringing steadily for a quarter of a century and, in particular, since the 1987 crash.

Trying to describe the catastrophic swings observed over such a long period throughout the Single Market, Mandelbrot introduced multifractal time and thus ushered the history of finance into a dynamic world, where stock market trading time no longer has anything in common with physical time, since, in this new model, 'trading time speeds up the clock in periods of high volatility, and slows it down in periods of stability',[1] the space of fractal geometry combining here with the 'multifractal' chronometry of the fourth dimension.

With our professor emeritus, then, it is no longer just 'critical space' that is heralded, but the effraction of History, the 'critical spacetime' of times to come!

With Benoit Mandelbrot, then, property bubbles suddenly turn into FINANCIAL

1 *Ibid.*, p. 22.

MANDELBUBBLES, not just within the expanse of real estate, but also within time, the long durations of the 'world economy' so dear to Fernand Braudel.

Strangely, we note yet again that the 'loop' and the 'sphere' shoot to the fore, as though the circular time of days gone by was reasserting its rights over the linear time of a Progress once continuous . . .

After Karl Popper's famous 'feedback loops', Carlo Rovelli, as we've just seen, now introduces his 'loop quantum gravity'.

Circular time yesterday, linear time of progress right now, and tomorrow, or soon after no doubt, thanks to Mandelbrot, globalitarian time . . . Here TIME – from the Latin *tempus*, which referred to a 'fraction of duration' as distinct from *aevum*, which was used of continuity and of an 'era' – really is the ACCIDENT TO END ALL ACCIDENTS. This is because 'multifractal' effraction of the durations involved in stock exchange operations tallies with Heisenberg's uncertainty principle, only to be applied to the modellers, the financial planners in a finance industry that has gone algorithmic, the famous credit crunch of the market here signalling the end of an era, the BIG CRUNCH of turbocapitalism!

As an academic recently pointed out: 'We must finally have the humility to say that we can't model uncertainty accurately.' And to add, as far as I'm concerned, that, despite the propaganda of Progress, confidence never will be automatic!

But let's get back to Karl Popper and his indeterminism. According to Popper, and his 'feedback loops', events influence our opinions every bit as much as these same opinions influence events. But the acceleration of the real, of real time, is turning our situation on its head, since, from now on, it is accidents and not just events anymore that influence our deep feelings. And this has reached the point where the community of opinion of our mutual interests is now taken over by the 'community of emotion' of the present instant, with emotional synchronization subsequently taking over from the standardization of public opinion that was, all the same, at the root of representative democracy.

And note how, with Mandelbrot, Karl Popper's 'feedback loop' just keeps on shrinking, like some *peau de chagrin*, with the accruing risks that this implies for the survival of our old political parties, now literally overtaken at speed, much like economic investors. The systemic crash under way since 2007 affects the political top brass of the Republic every bit as much as those of the big banks in a market that's interconnected thanks to twenty-first century program trading, with the high-frequency electronic platforms of the flash trading that was responsible for the CYBERCRASH of 6 May 2010 functioning outside human time, thanks to the *time machine* of Stock Exchange computers.

But, here, we are in the presence of an absence – in other words, of an object contrary to objectivity. In actual fact, if time is no more, if it is disappearing into its acceleration, INSTABILITY is brought to a head, and the moment of inertia of interactive CONNECTION dominates, on all sides now, the inertia of PLACES, the inertia of fixity as well as of immobility.

Hannah Arendt put it forcefully: 'Instability is a functional prerequisite of total domination.' Well, what can we say about the instability of the instantaneity of real time? Are we going to have to live (survive), tomorrow, under the domination of a sort of *tribunal d'instance*, a court that would rule on the instant? On this tyranny of time or, rather, lack of time, involved in the exodus of free will and democracy, with everyone affected by an instability at once psycho- and loco-motive due to our hypermotivity – in other words to our loss of control over our vital reflexes? For, by then these will be conditioned by the flows, the inflows, of a cybernetic environment that will soon be uninhabitable.

Circuit, short-circuit – let's go back now to the circle, the *kuklos*, and this circular particle accelerator, the CYCLOTRON, which is at the origins of nuclear physics, having been invented at Berkeley in the early 1930s and which suddenly, in 2009, turned into an underground CATHEDRAL, the temple of an accelerating epic science launched in quest of 'God's particle', this HADRON that is still missing from the collections of the savants of contemporary physics.

Note firstly that the cosmotheist venture in question started, beneath the roots of the tree of knowledge of Judeo-Christian genesis, with the original accident, the break-down of a 'reality-accelerator' that was supposed to discover, at the end of a tunnel, the infinitesimal particle at the origins of astrophysics. All this should alert us to the megalomania of a science deprived of a critical conscience and coupled with a sort of megaloscopy of the infinitely small, whereby the LARGE HADRON COLLIDER of Geneva claims to reveal – live – the creation of the world, no less, at the obvious risk of procreating a 'black hole' – of low amplitude, they say, no doubt to reassure us about the risks being run.

Those risks have sparked legal proceedings instituted by sundry American physicists and other theorists of chaos, such as Otto Rössler from Göttingen University, against their CERN colleagues.

In this 'speedway' where the landscape is the lack of a landscape, the exodus of the speed of light actually leads to a crash of reason, of 'common sense'. What then surges up, *ex abrupto*, is the Accident in Time triggered by a physics that is now the victim of a coma affecting all knowledge acquired here below.

An accident in substances, an accident in distances, an accident in knowledge. In the end, Rimbaud was right: 'We've got it back. What? Eternity.' Indeed, if time is disappearing completely as an adjustment variable necessary to the space of the NANOWORLD that surrounds us, the eternal present of relativism will soon reign supreme as of right, to the detriment of the cumbersome processes of History.

It is odd, all the same, to see that though the astrophysicists of exobiology appear to believe in universal life spread throughout outer space, they still refuse to believe in life everlasting!

'O ye hypocrites, ye can discern the face of the sky, but can ye not discern the signs of the times?' (Matthew 16:3). This phrase of Christ's seems to be directed at today's global climate change ecologists who strangely leave out grey ecology, the sudden retention of spacetime, the temporal compression of the common world, even as those cosmologists who are devotees of the BIG BANG envisage, most concretely, the hypothesis of the BIG CRUNCH, the final contraction of the expanding Universe.

Fifteen billion years ago, according to the late Belgian astronomer-physicist abbé Lemaître, Russian cosmologist-physicist George Gamow and company, there would have been a deflagration of the primordial atom, triggering the expansion of a bubble that was to keep growing all the way along an – astro-historical

– continuum right up to the BIG CRUNCH –
the implosion and crash of the Time Barrier. But
today we're forced to report that in their quest
to discover the very first second of the creation
of the Universe, our savvy astronomers of the
vastness of outer space seem particularly anxious
about the infinitesimal duration of the initial
instant.[1]

That quest first gave us the cyclotron; then the
US laboratory FERMILAB built a six-kilometre
atomic racetrack known as the TEVATRON;
and now, finally, we have Europe's LARGE
HADRON COLLIDER, 27 kilometres long.
The name is significant since we've gone from
the invention of the ACCELERATOR – linear
then circular – to the COLLIDER, the impact
study of the speed of light concluding with the
spectacular smashing of the Time Barrier!

A fine illustration of the accident to end all
accidents in this brand of time which certain
physicists are asking us to forget completely –
Copernican astronomy of the 'telescopic' origins
of the conquest of space leading, in Geneva, to

1 Hubert Reeves, *The Latest News from the Cosmos*, tr. Donald
Winkler. Toronto: Stoddart Kids, 1997.

the 'telescoping', the major collision, of the end of time!

Science, the BIG SCIENCE of physics, is not, in actual fact, at peace with itself. It is at war with time: 'the stately slowness of duration, the moving wonder of every hour', is the way Impressionism and its phenomenologists put it, Claude Monet among them. In so doing, between 1899 and 1901, they prefigured the theory of relativity, Albert Einstein's theory about point of view. Monet, the man who painted the celebrated 'Series' even decreed that: EVERYTHING CHANGES, EVEN STONE, thereby forecasting the emergence of kinematic energy alongside kinetic energy. The Lumière Brothers would develop kinematic energy more fully, thereby anticipating the mutations, in the twentieth century, of the multifractal spacetime of which Mandelbrot – that other impressionist! – would become the secular prophet.

But let's go back once more to the Geneva temple, this cyclindrical Plato's cave, where the illuminists of the Last Day keep the flame of Progress alive behind the 'scientific truth' that Einstein, that apostle of general relativity, abhorred.

It really is weird the way the significance of such a *camera obscura*, this cathedral crypt buried beneath the border between two countries, has never got our savants thinking, with the exception of those mentioned above. How can it be that such an edifice, the cost of which comes close to the billions lost by a certain trader who had the media in a tizz for quite a few months in 2010, only ever attracted the sarcastic remarks of scientific popularizers targeting anyone who might be worried about it, just as the great breakdown that crowned the CERN collider's unveiling was met only with silence on the part of admirers of epic science?

The damage done by COSMOTHEISM here matches the damage done by a form of fanatical sun worship in which the accelerating speed of light illuminates history, in anticipation of human sacrifices quite different from the people who got burned in astronomical financial investments, for the edification of these temples of illusion – like the one recently proposed for Beijing. This one will be 'an international linear collider' and, to put it in a nutshell, it will be allied to the crash tests of an automobile industry in crisis, inside the little cubbyhole of a NANOWORLD where the world's ecological footprint now leads, directly, to the integral accident in public finances . . .

In the same vein, in 2010 China made a conspicuous entrance in second place in the Supercomputer Top 500 List, just behind the United States, thanks to a motor named NEBULAE. Its performance benchmark is 1.27 petaflops, which translates as the capacity to effect 1.27 million billion operations per second, whereas Jaguar, the computer in the US Energy Department in Tennessee, can achieve 1.75 petaflops. Forecast for 2020 is a 'great accelerator calculator' that will be able to attain an exoflop – or a billion billion operations per second.

We might remember that these motors are used in scientific research, in genetic sequencing, but especially in the strategic domain touching on national sovereignty.[1]

According to the specialists, the field of application of supercomputing never stops getting bigger. So, geophysicists today are able to predict, in real time, the aftershocks that follow an earthquake.[2] On the other hand, they are currently

1 *Le Monde*, 26 June 2010.
2 *Ibid.*

unable to anticipate the fatal consequences of a CYBERCRASH of great magnitude affecting the whole of the financial system. Yet, it's only too easy to foresee that the automation involved in high-frequency flash trading will lead, tomorrow, to the INTEGRAL ACCIDENT in very-high-frequency high finance!

In this endless race, the future Great Profit Collider will no doubt lead to the discovery, right at the end of the tunnel of History, of the 'primordial atom' of stocks, for a financial industry in the process of accelerated automation and this, to the detriment of financial agents who are so incredibly unscrupulous and dangerous, as proved by 'Kafka's Trial' – sorry, that was Kerviel, the guilty trader from French bank, Société générale.

According to both the *Times* and the *Daily Telegraph*, reporting in mid-September 2008, one of the four detectors in CERN's Great Collider was broken into by intruders who successfully hacked into the LARGE HARDON COLLIDER's computer network as early as Wednesday 8 September, the day Geneva's underground cathedral was officially set in motion. We might also recall that on 22 September, the newspaper

Libération announced that the LHC had come to a standstill, after breaking down during a test run conducted on Friday 17 September of the same year, a year that was to see the Wall Street Barrier come crashing down.

Index